# 10

## Things I Know
## About Penguins

Written by
Wendy Wax and Della Rowland

With Illustrations by
Thomas Payne

## A CALICO BOOK

Published by Contemporary Books, Inc.
CHICAGO • NEW YORK

Library of Congress Cataloging-in-Publication Data

Wax, Wendy.
    10 things I know about penguins / written by Wendy Wax and Della
    Rowland : illustrated by Thomas Payne.
            p.    cm.
    "A Calico book."
    Summary: A simple introduction to those lovable birds that live in
    Antarctica and parts of nearby countries.
    ISBN 0-8092-4349-0
    1. Penguins—Juvenile literature.  [1. Penguins.]   I. Rowland,
    Della.   II. Payne, Tom, ill.   III. Title.   IV. Title: Ten things I
    know about penguins.
    QL696.S473W39    1989
    596.4'41—dc19                                          88-37549
                                                                CIP
                                                                AC

Photos courtesy of Animals Animals/Earth Scenes: Zig Leszczynski, pages
4–5, 9; G. L. Kooyman, pages 6, 16–17; Fritz Prenzel, page 11; E. A.
O'Connell, page 12; OSF/D. Allan, page 14; OSF/B. Osborne, page 15.
Photos courtesy of Photo Researchers: William R. Curtsinger, pages 3, 18;
George Holton, page 11; Roger Tory Peterson, pages 11, 18.
Cover photo courtesy of Black Star, M. P. Kahl.

# 10

## Things I Know
## About Penguins

Most penguins live in
Antarctica and parts of nearby
countries. They like to live where
it is icy cold.

**1**

2

Penguins are birds that swim
instead of fly.
They use their wings like
flippers underwater.

Penguins spend most of their time
in the water looking for food.
Some can stay underwater
without breathing for one hour.

3

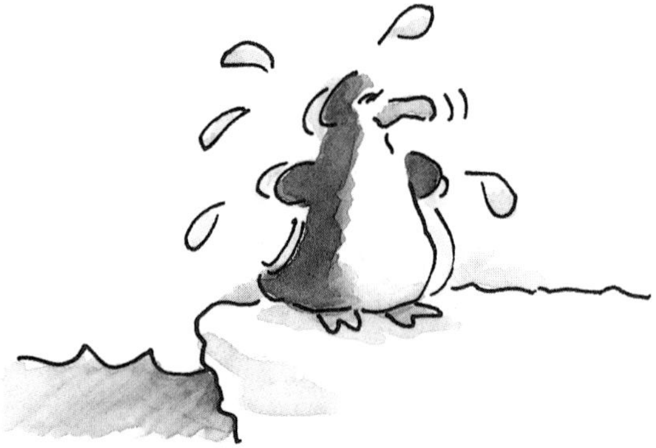

# 4

The penguin's thick, oily feathers are
warm and waterproof.

There are eighteen different kinds of penguins. The blue fairy penguin is only one foot tall, while the emperor penguin stands four feet tall.

Once a year,
most kinds of penguins make nests and
lay their eggs.

HI POP!

**7**

Instead of making a nest,
the male emperor penguin holds
an egg on its feet to keep
it warm until it hatches.

Penguins eat fish.
When the penguin chicks are first hatched,
the adults chew up their food for them.

8

HEY mom!

Penguins live in large groups
called rookeries. Sometimes
one million birds live in one rookery.

# 10

On land, penguins travel
by waddling or hopping on their
short legs. When they are
in a hurry, they slide on their bellies.